How to Draw
Cartoons

HOW TO DRAW CARTOONS

BY SYD HOFF

SCHOLASTIC INC.
New York Toronto London Auckland Sydney

ISBN 0-590-40689-2

Selections From *Jokes To Enjoy, Draw And Tell*, copyright © 1974 by Syd Hoff. Additional text and illustrations in this edition copyright © 1975 by Syd Hoff. This edition is published by Scholastic Book Services, a division of Scholastic Inc., 730 Broadway, New York, NY 10003, by arrangements with G. P. Putnam's Sons, publishers of *Jokes To Enjoy, Draw And Tell*, and with Syd Hoff.

12 11 10 9 8 7 6 5 4   9/8 0 1/9

Let's start out
by drawing a face.
Faces are usually
round, aren't they?
So—

draw a circle.

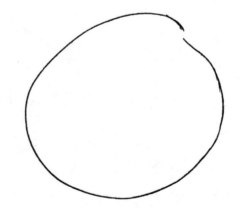

Now add eyes

and a nose

and a mouth.
You have made a face!

You can do a lot
of things with a face.

Add hair,
and make a lady!

Add a mustache,
and make a man!

You can give the
lady a double chin
and earrings.

You can put a hat
on the man.

*If you can't
draw a circle,
you can make
faces any shape.*

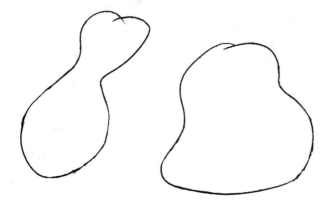

For instance—

Men's faces...

Ladies' faces.

Now let's make expressions.

People can be glad.

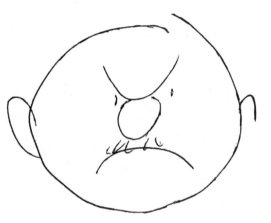

People can be mad

People can laugh.

People can cry.

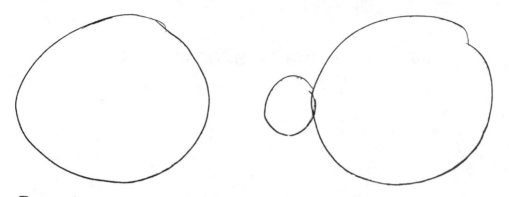

People can turn and show you their profiles, too. So, draw a circle again, and this time add another little circle next to it.

Now make a
lady's profile.

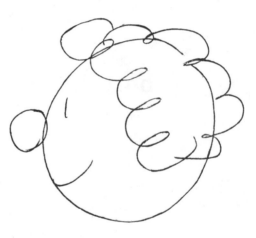

Now make a
man's profile.

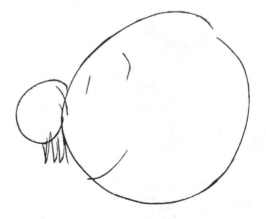

*Profiles can be
any shape, too.*

Now let's make figures,
because faces can't walk around
without them.

The average figure is five and a half
heads tall.

Shoulders are just below the head and neck.

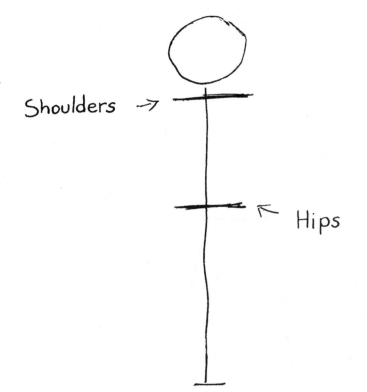

Shoulders →

← Hips

Hips are about halfway down the length of the figure.

Now add two arms and two legs.

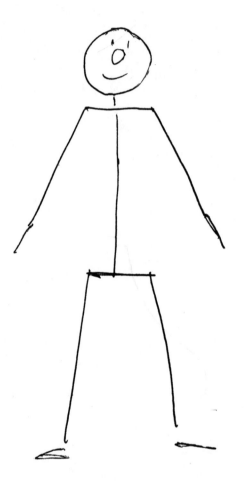

This is called a stick figure.

Let's make our
stick figure
bend his knees.

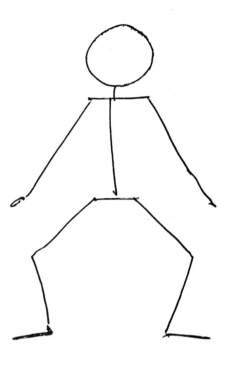

Let's make him
bend his arms.

Now he can walk!

He can run!

He can jump!

He can do anything
we please!

Now let's put some
weight on our
stick figures.

Make them fat!

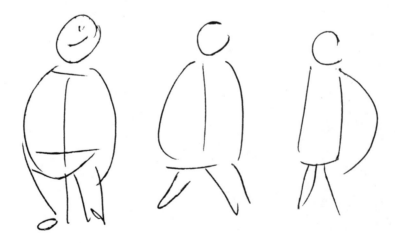

Put them on a diet!

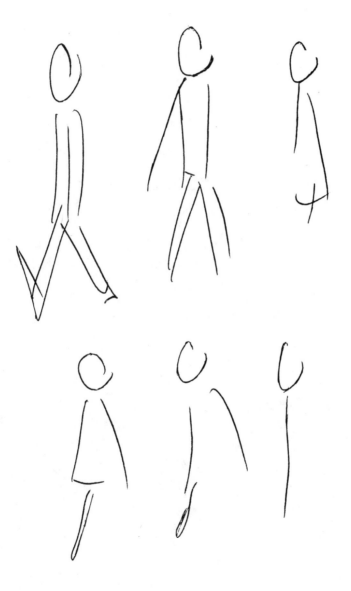

Make one lollipop.

Make two lollipops.

Now make a
mouse!

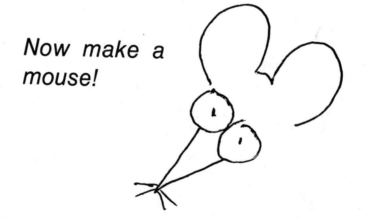

Make an ice cream cone.

Make a bird!

Make an ice cream cone upside down.

Make a clown!

Draw an arrow.

Draw another arrow.

Draw a cat!

Draw a straight line.

Draw a curved line.

Draw a dog!

Draw the dog
chasing
the cat.

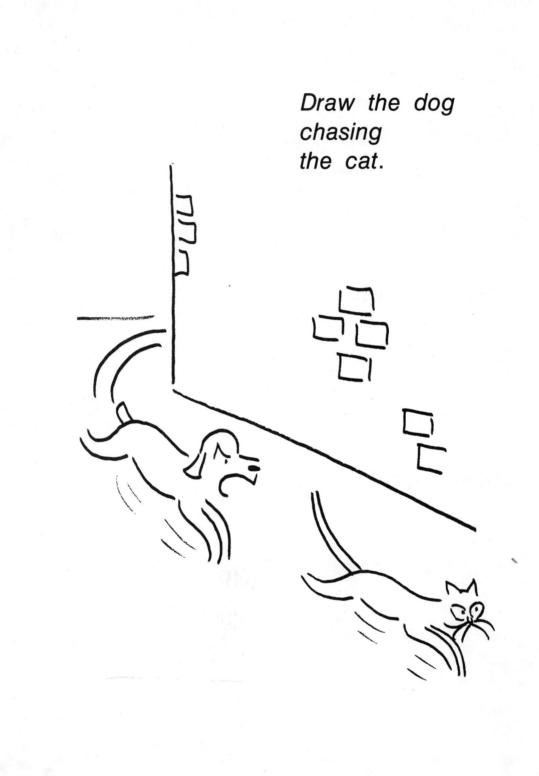

*Draw
the cat
up in
a
tree!*

Draw a grape.

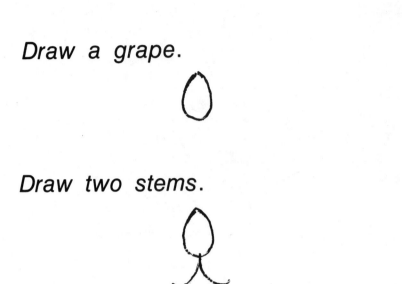

Draw two stems.

Draw a lioness!

Draw some lines.

Draw a lion!

Draw two doughnuts.

Draw a line.

Draw a racing car.

*Draw yourself in the
racing car–*

and go for a ride!

Now draw a policeman pointing to a sign!